The Bunny Kit

Alicia Merrett

A · THOMAS · DUNNE · BOOK

ST. MARTIN'S
PRESS
NEW YORK

A QUARTO BOOK

"A Thomas Dunne Book"

ISBN 0-312-13447-9

This book was designed and produced by
Quarto Inc, The Old Brewery, 6 Blundell Street,
London N7 9BH

Designer Debbie Mole • **Senior editor** Kate Kirby •
Editor Barbara Cheney • **Senior art editor** Julie Francis •
Photographers Laura Wickenden, Colin Bowling •
Illustrations Elsa Godfrey • **Picture researcher**
Susannah Jayes • **Picture manager** Giulia Hetherington •
Art director Moira Clinch • **Editorial director** Mark
Dartford

Typeset by Central Southern Typesetters, Eastbourne
Bunny components supplied by Regent Publishing Services
Ltd, Hong Kong
Manufactured in China. Assembled and printed in
China by Regent Publishing Services Ltd.

With thanks to Kathi Campbell of Heart to Hand of
Encinitas, CA, who supplied the "Honey Bunny" featured on
page 47 of the bunny gallery.

Contents

About bunnies

There are famous rabbits – Peter, the Velveteen Rabbit, Bugs, Br'er, Thumper, and Rabbit in the Pooh books – these are rabbits who fire the imagination, beloved by generations of children.

There are pet rabbits who live in hutches in suburban backyards feasting on chickweed, dandelion, dock, and lettuce, and there are their cousins who board at schools and are taken home in the long vacations by first-graders.

There are dear soft toy rabbits suspended above a baby's crib or sharing a child's pillow, watching over little ones while they sleep. There are old rabbits whose charges have grown up and left the nursery; these old friends are often moth-eaten or well-chewed, sometimes venerated, sometimes consigned to the bottom of toy boxes or the back of closets – rest homes for stuffed toys the world over.

There is the cuddly bunny contained in this kit. It will repay the love you put into its making by being a faithful companion and friend to you or to whomever you choose to give it to.

In this kit, you will find the patterns and step-by-step instructions to make a caramel-colored bunny which stands on its hind legs, and all the materials needed to make it. There are also patterns and instructions for making some clothes – a coat, a reversible vest, and an apron – and accessories such as a bow tie and vegetables.

Bunny maker's basic kit

You won't need specialized tools to make the bunny in this kit, and probably nothing that isn't already in your sewing basket.

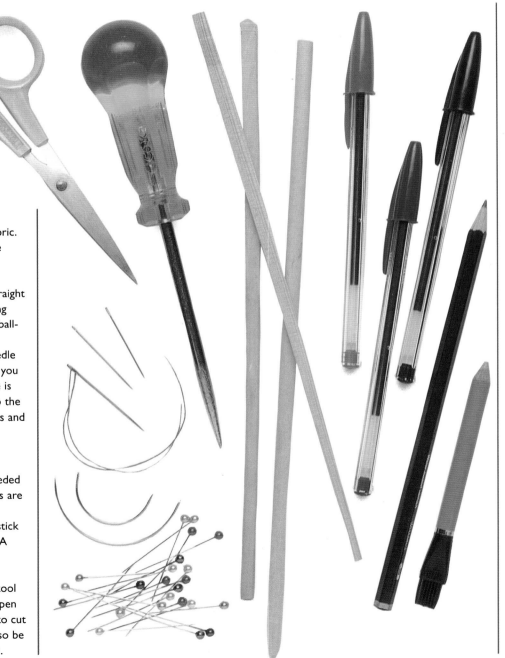

The basic kit

Small, pointed scissors For cutting the fur fabric. Always cut the back of the fabric, pulling the pile apart as you go to avoid cutting the fur fibers.

Sewing machine Machine stitching makes the seams much stronger than hand sewing. Only straight stitch is required. Use cotton or polyester sewing thread and size 14 (90) needles, preferably the "ball-point" type recommended for stretch fabrics.

Hand-sewing needles Use an embroidery needle (the eye is larger) with doubled strong thread if you stitch the bunny by hand. A small curved needle is strongly recommended for stitching the limbs to the body, and a normal sewing needle for the clothes and accessories.

Pins Use colored-head pins, so they are clearly visible in the fur.

Awl or thick knitting needle This will be needed for making holes in the fur fabric where the eyes are going to go.

Stuffing tools A wooden stick, such as a chopstick or a dowel with a tapered end, is most suitable. A thick knitting needle can be used, but it is very slippery and harder to control.

Marking tools A sharp, soft pencil is the best tool to mark the patterns on the fabrics. A ballpoint pen makes a clear mark, but on light fabrics be sure to cut just inside the line. Other fabric markers may also be suitable; try them first on a spare piece of fabric.

Fabrics and fillings

Fur fabrics

The best fur fabrics are man-made acrylics with a knitted back. Look for a soft texture and dense pile (as in the kit). Bunnies can be made in different colors, for example white, grey, brown, black, etc. Some suitable color swatches are shown left.

Lining and pad fabrics

• Thin, soft acrylic fleece is the most appropriate (pink samples).
• Some thick stretch fabrics or brushed nylon can also be used (white sample).
• Felt can be used, but is not recommended because it is not very strong (peach and brown samples).

Other fabrics

Bunny can also be made in other fabrics although the shape may be slightly different. Firm woven cotton fabrics – plain, print or plaid – are suitable, and a bunny made in a velvet-type fabric looks good. Leave extra allowances when using fabrics that are liable to fray.

Fillings

<u>Polyester</u> Best when springy and bulky. Choose good quality white stuffing (supplied in kit).
<u>Rice</u> Similar to plastic pellets (see below). Not suitable for children.
<u>Plastic pellets</u> Give a beanbag effect. Not suitable for children's toys.
<u>Kapok</u> Not recommended (not illustrated). It is not bulky enough as it compresses with wear; and some people are allergic to it.

Bunny features

Features animate soft toys, giving them character. The Kit Bunny comes with plastic safety eyes, lids, and a nose, and embroidery thread for the mouth. You can add other touches such as whiskers and embroidered teeth; instructions are given on this page.

Plastic safety eyes Strongly recommended. Once they have been inserted, they cannot be removed, making them safe for children's toys. They have to be attached to the head before it is stuffed, using a fastener which is either plastic (as in the kit) or metal. Colors can be brown, black, amber, or pink (some rabbits have pink eyes). The eyes come in sizes ranging from ⅜ inch to 1½ inches; the most common sizes are ½ inch, ⁹⁄₁₆ inch, and ⅝ inch. Instructions for fastening the eyes are given in the Bunny Features section on page 18. Eyes can be used on their own, or in the case of bunnies they can be used in conjunction with plastic lids (see below).

Plastic lids These have holes to put the shank of the eye through, which is then pushed through a hole in the fur and fastened as normal. Sometimes their shape is asymmetrical, to make a left and right eye.

Noses Bunnies have small triangular noses, usually pink. Plastic pink triangular safety noses are fastened in the same way as the eyes. Alternatively, the nose can be simply represented with two straight stitches in the shape of a V, or embroidered with satin stitch in pink thread (see below).

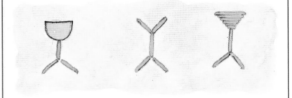

Mouths Take a straight stitch in pink thread down the center of the nose and then into an inverted V (see above).

Whiskers Sisal string is good; cut a length and unravel the fibers. Transparent nylon thread, and normal sewing or embroidery thread can also be used. Thread a few at a time on a large-eyed needle and stitch across under nose. Knot in place. Whiskers are not safe for children.

Teeth As a finishing touch, embroider Bunny's two big white front teeth with a few long stitches in thick white embroidery thread.

Threads and stitches

Threads

For stitching the bunny, choose a color to match the main fur. Stitches are not very visible as they disappear in the pile.

Cotton or polyester mixtures, size 50 For machine sewing. Strong or buttonhole thread For closing openings and assembling. Embroidery thread In pink for embroidering the mouth (supplied in kit).

Stitches

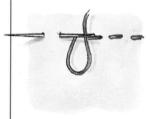

Running stitch Used for gathering fabric. Take several small and even stitches through the point of the needle before pulling it through the fabric.

Backstitch Holds fabric layers together firmly. Take one stitch on the line. For the next stitch, go back on the line, push the needle in, and come out one short space ahead of the previous one.

Ladder stitch Used for invisible joining. Take small, even stitches, with each stitch taken on the opposite side of the seam (for closing openings), or alternating between a limb and the body (for joining limbs).

Basting Joins fabric layers temporarily. Use a contrasting color thread to make running stitches between ¼ inch and ⅜ inch long.

Straight embroidery stitches Used for the mouth and nose.

Satin stitch Useful for embroidering noses. Make straight stitches very close together.

Machine stitching gives strength to seams. But you can sew the Bunny by hand, provided you make close stitches and use strong double thread.

A bunny is a popular toy with children, so it must comply with all the safety standards. Toy safety regulations are very stringent, and makers have to be conversant with them. Here we give some general guidelines.

Safety first

To be suitable for children
• Fabrics and stuffings have to be of low flammability, non-allergenic, and non-toxic.
• Eyes and noses must not break easily and must be attached in such a way that they will not come off.
• All stitching in the toy has to be firm and well anchored so that seams will not split open. For this reason, machine stitching is recommended.
• Materials should be purchased from reputable dealers who can give reliable information regarding their safety.
• If you are making bunnies to sell, check the regulations carefully beforehand.

Supplied in your
Bunny kit are the
following items:

**Caramel fur
fabric**
• 12 x 21^1/$_2$ inches
White fur fabric
• 3^1/$_8$ x 12^1/$_2$ inches
White fleece
• 4 x 8 inches
Eyes
• A pair, ^{1}/$_2$-inch,
plastic safety, with
fasteners, and a
pair of lids to
match
Nose
• Triangular, ^{3}/$_4$-inch,
pink, plastic safety,
with fastener
Thread
• 1 yard pink
embroidery thread
for mouth
Filling
• 4 ounces
polyester
Ribbon
(For the bow tie)
• 11 inches
Thin elastic
• 6 inches

Making your Bunny

**This sweet hug-me, love-me bunny, complete with
stylish bow tie, is waiting to be cuddled and
cosseted. Make it for yourself following the
instructions in this section, or – if you can bear to
part with it – as a companion to a young friend.
Patterns can be reused to make a whole family of
bunnies in plush furs or different fabrics.**

Preparing the pattern

Trace or photocopy the pattern pieces (shown here full size). Follow the pattern pieces chart, making duplicate pieces as needed, turning pieces over to obtain a reversed pattern piece for those that require it. Transfer all markings to the pattern pieces. For durability a glue paper pieces to cardboard before cutting the shapes.

From caramel fur fabric
Outer ears
• 2
Head gusset
• 1
Side heads
• 2, one reversed
Side bodies
• 2, one reversed
Arms
• 4, two reversed
Legs
• 4, two reversed
Tail
• 1

From white fur fabric
Body gusset
• 1
Tail
• 1

From white fleece
Inner ears
• 2
Foot pads
• 2

Seam allowances of ¼ inch are included in the patterns.

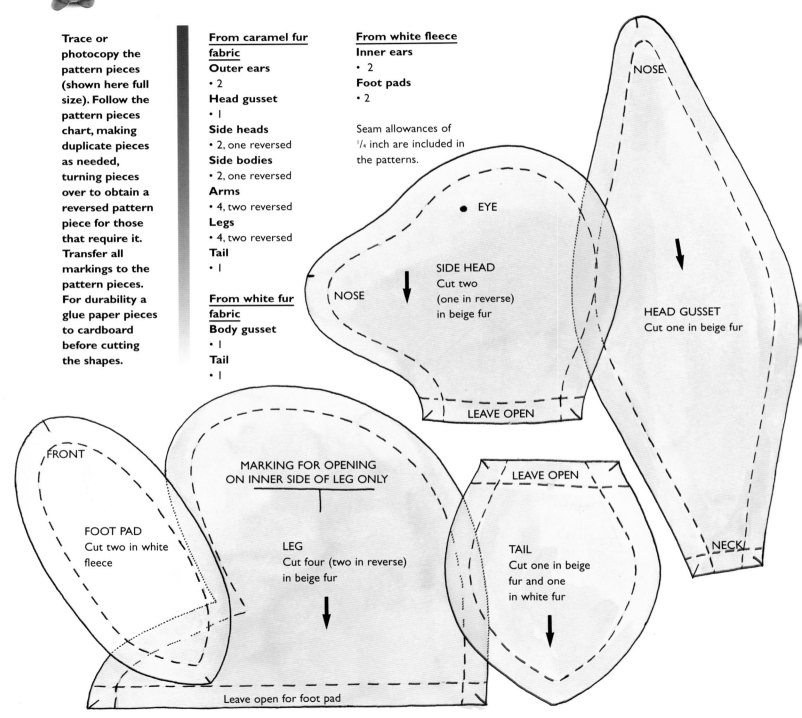

NOSE

EYE

SIDE HEAD
Cut two
(one in reverse)
in beige fur

NOSE

LEAVE OPEN

NOSE

HEAD GUSSET
Cut one in beige fur

NECK

FRONT

FOOT PAD
Cut two in white fleece

MARKING FOR OPENING
ON INNER SIDE OF LEG ONLY

LEG
Cut four (two in reverse)
in beige fur

Leave open for foot pad

LEAVE OPEN

TAIL
Cut one in beige
fur and one
in white fur

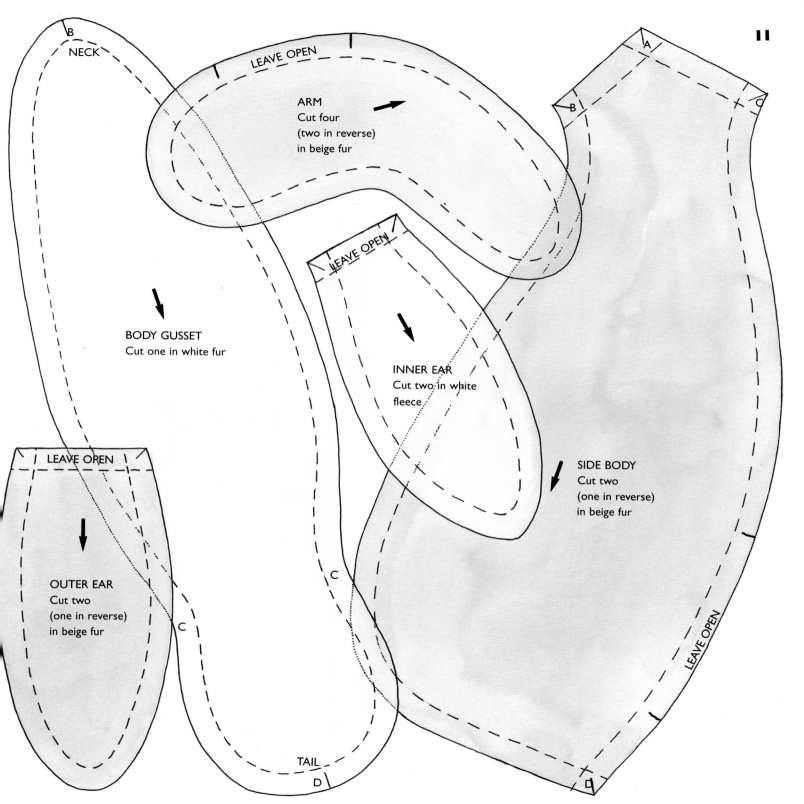

The amount of fabric provided does not allow for errors, so make sure all the pattern pieces are in the positions shown in the photograph before proceeding to mark or cut. Use small, pointed scissors to cut the fur, and a soft pencil, ballpoint pen, or dressmakers' chalk to mark the fabric.

1 Pinning on pattern
Establish the direction of the pile of the fur fabrics by stroking them. Turn them over face down on the table and mark the direction of the pile with arrows on the back. Place the cardboard patterns or pin the paper pattern pieces on the back of the corresponding fabric, the arrows on the pattern pieces pointing in the same direction as the arrows marked on the fabric.

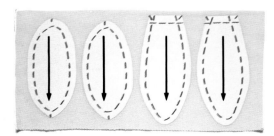

2 Place the foot pad and inner ear patterns on the back of the fleece, as above.

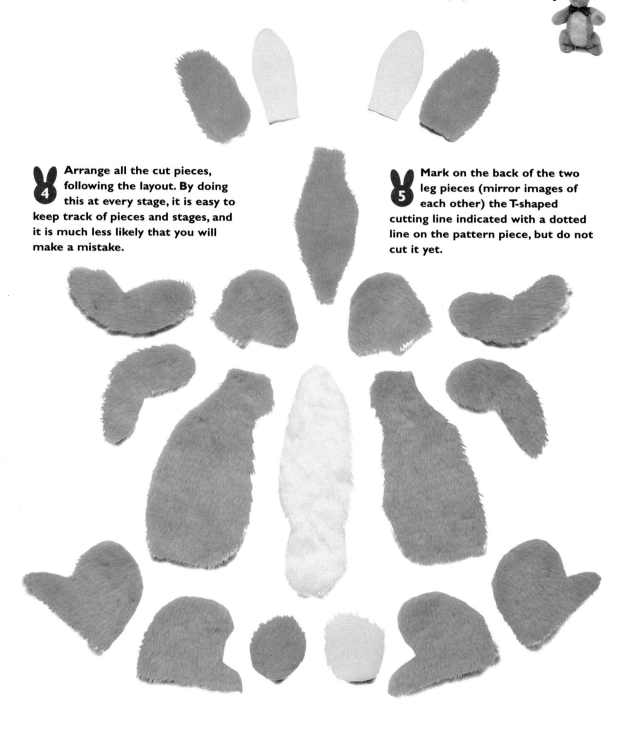

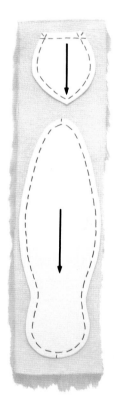

🐰 **4** Arrange all the cut pieces, following the layout. By doing this at every stage, it is easy to keep track of pieces and stages, and it is much less likely that you will make a mistake.

🐰 **5** Mark on the back of the two leg pieces (mirror images of each other) the T-shaped cutting line indicated with a dotted line on the pattern piece, but do not cut it yet.

🐰 **3** <u>Marking and cutting</u> Mark around the patterns on the fur and fleece fabrics and transfer all the markings. Remove the pattern pieces and pins (if used) and cut the fabrics: for the furs, slip the point of the scissors under the pile and snip the back of the fabric. The pile will pull apart easily afterward.

Pinning the pieces

Putting the right sides together, match and pin the pieces, pushing the pile to the inside. In most cases, pins will be strong enough to hold the pieces while you stitch them by hand or machine, although basting before stitching is recommended in a few cases.

2 **Ears** Place inner and outer ear pieces right sides together to make two ears. Pin around the long curved edges. Leave the short sides open.

1 **Head** Join the two side heads, right sides together. Pin from the nose to the neck only.

3 **Arms** Pin the arm pieces right sides together, leaving an opening for each arm.

4 **Legs** Place the leg pieces right sides together, and pin around the curved edges for each leg. Leave the lower straight edge open to insert the foot pads later.

6 **Body pieces** Place the two body pieces right sides together, and pin the short seam from the neck from **A** to **B**, and then the back seam from **C** to **D**. Leave an opening in the lower back as indicated.

5 **Tail** Pin the tail pieces – one caramel, one white – right sides together, leaving the short straight edge open.

Sewing the pieces

Ears The inner ear is slightly smaller than the outer ear and needs to be stretched to fit.

2 Eyes Mark the eye position on the right side of the fabric with a stitch in colored thread, leaving an end on the right side.

6 Fur fabric is slippery, so check to make sure the stitching does not go too close to the edge of the piece on the other side.

5 Careful pinning and stitching should prevent one side of the fur fabric from slipping along the other side.

3 Sewing fur An opening in the back of the leg is not necessary; as an opening will be cut in the side later.

4 Ballpoint machine needles are highly recommended, as they are specially designed for knitted fabrics.

Set your sewing machine to stitch the fur fabric, using needle size 14 (90), and straight stitch size $2\frac{1}{2}$. Test your stitching on scraps of fur fabric before starting to stitch the bunny. Use colored thread to match the caramel fabric – the stitches will disappear in the pile and will not be seen in the white sections. Leave a seam allowance of $\frac{1}{4}$ inch. If you prefer to stitch by hand, make close stitches and use strong doubled thread. Remove the pins as you sew.

Joining the pieces

The next stage is to join the pieces together. Follow these instructions carefully. Bunny is starting to take shape.

1 **Head** Join the head gusset to the head sides. Starting at the nose end, pin along each seam to the point where the gusset gets wider – about 1½ inches. Leaving a small gap in the center for the nose shank; baste and hand stitch the two seams. (See detail, left.)

2 Continue to pin, baste, and stitch the two head side seams to the back of the neck. Leave the lower part of the neck open.

3 **Body** Match the top of the body gusset to the center neck seam of the body at its lower point. Pin the gusset around to the center and lower edges of the body sides - no openings are needed here. Baste if necessary.

5 **Legs** Cut the T-shaped markings on just two sides of the legs using small, pointed scissors. Check you are cutting on the "mirror image" side of the legs, and take care not to cut through to the other side. (See detail, above right.)

4 **Foot pads** Pin foot pads to lower feet openings, matching front of pad with front foot seam. It is recommended that you baste this seam before stitching. (See detail, above.)

Sew and turn

Ears As the inner ear piece is smaller than the outer, the fur will be pulled slightly inward, giving a good finish.

2 **Eyes** The ends of colored thread for marking the eyes should be clearly visible from the outside. If they are not, mark them again.

3 **Nose** Use your stuffing tool or the end of a pencil to push out the nose seam.

Machine or hand stitch all the pinned and basted pieces with a seam allowance of $1/4$ inch as before. Make sure you remove all the pins, and that the pile of the fur is pushed in. Turn all the pieces right side out, and gently push out all the seams with your stuffing tool to check they are all firm and even.

4 **Seams** Use a thick needle to tease out fur that gets caught in the seams, particularly on the tail, the foot pads, and the ears, where caramel and white fabrics are joined together.

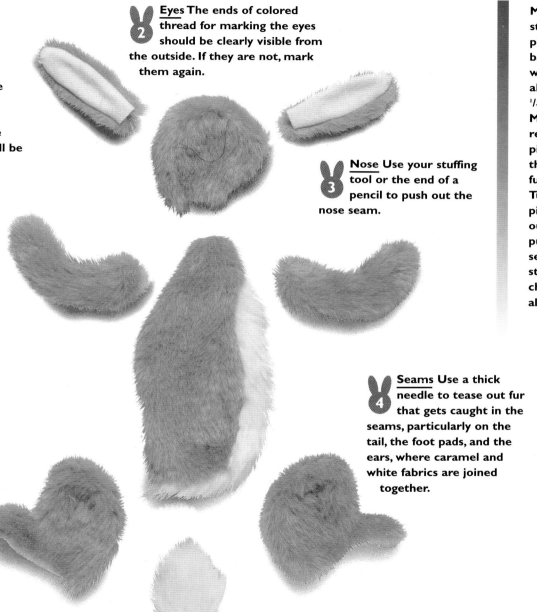

Creating the features

It is the facial features of your bunny which will give it character, so take special care during this part of the procedure. Remember that rabbits' eyes are on the sides of the head, giving them a wide field of view, to detect predators. For safety reasons, the eye and nose fasteners must fit very tightly. Securing the fasteners is a fiddly operation and needs to be taken carefully and slowly; immersing fasteners in hot water for 30 seconds makes them easier to insert. Once attached, they cannot be removed.

1 **Eyes** Using the placement points as guidelines, check that they are positioned evenly on the sides of the head. Adjust if necessary.

2 Fit each eye into a plastic eyelid. Make sure they will go in the correct right or left position.

3 Make holes in the two eye positions with an awl or a thick knitting needle. Remove the thread markers. Slip the shank of each eye through, and secure firmly from the inside with the safety fastener disk, which should fit like a "hat" over the shank.

4 **Nose** Slip the shank of the nose through the gap left in the nose seam. Make sure the nose is in the correct position, the point of the triangle down. Attach the fastening disk as described in step 5.

5 **Technique for attaching the fasteners** Immerse fasteners in hot water for 30 seconds before attaching them to nose or eyes. Press each fastener as far as it will go by hand; then slip an empty spool over the shank and tap lightly with a hammer until the shank shows three ridges.

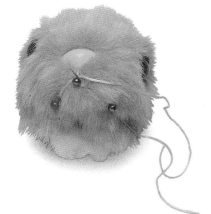

6 <u>Mouth</u> Stuff the head very firmly, but do not close. Thread a long darning needle with the pink embroidery thread doubled. Bring the needle in from the neck, through the stuffing, and out as near as possible to the lower point of the nose. Embroider the mouth as shown in the illustration.

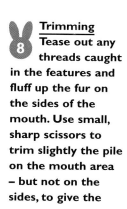

7 **Ears** Fold lower edges of the ears toward the inside center, and secure with a few stitches. Place them on the head with the whites of the inner ears facing out from the sides. Pin the ears on each side of the head, just below the gusset seam, and 1 inch behind the eye; work with both at the same time, so they can be spaced evenly. Compare them with the photograph of the finished bunny.

There is no need to turn up the lower edges.
Now stitch them in place with doubled strong thread and a long needle. Use ladder stitch, taking alternate stitches from the ear and the head, and stitch around three times for safety. The raw edges will be hidden by the seam. Release any fur trapped in the seams.

8 **Trimming** Tease out any threads caught in the features and fluff up the fur on the sides of the mouth. Use small, sharp scissors to trim slightly the pile on the mouth area – but not on the sides, to give the effect of whiskers – and also the fur in front of the eyes. Practice on a piece of scrap fur before making any cuts; you need to be confident in your trimming skills before tackling your bunny.

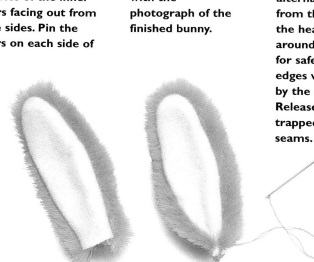

Stuffing and assembly

This final stage involves stuffing the bunny and attaching the head, arms, legs, and tail to the body. The head can be placed so that the bunny looks forward, or slightly to one side. Lay out the bunny pieces to make sure that nothing is missing. A curved needle is very helpful in the joining stages.

Arms Stuff each arm through the gap at the side; they need to be well filled, but not hard. Close the openings using ladder stitch.

Body Stuff the body firmly, first through the opening in the back, and then using the neck opening. Do not close either opening.

Legs Stuff each leg through the T-shaped opening, making sure you fill the toes and foot well, so the bunny can stand firmly on its feet. The sides should be stuffed relatively flat. Do not close the openings.

Tail Stuff lightly the top half of the tail only. Do not close the opening.

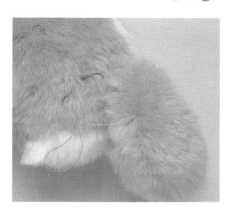

Attaching head to body Gently pull the head over the top of the neck so that it fits neatly, and pin in place. Use ladder stitch to secure the head onto the body, and stitch around three times for safety. Use your stuffing tool to make sure there is plenty of stuffing in the neck area to hold the head up. Add more stuffing through the back, if necessary, to give the rabbit a firm body. Close the back opening with ladder stitch.

Attaching arms Use ladder stitch to attach the arms firmly to the body, with the top of the arm about 1 inch down from the neck/body seam.

Attaching legs On a flat surface, position each leg so that the foot pads are level with each other so that the bunny can stand. Place the T-openings against each side of the body. Use ladder stitch to secure each leg to the body, stitching the open area in a round shape, so that the opening is well hidden. A curved needle is helpful.

Tail Position the tail at the base of the back between the two legs, point up and white side facing out. Use ladder stitch to attach the raw edges to the body, and again about 1½ inches higher up, leaving the top of the tail, the part that is stuffed, sticking out.

Finishing Tease out any fur trapped in seams. Your bunny is now ready and can be dressed in different ways (see overleaf) or finished with a bow tie (materials included in the kit; for assembly, see page 27).

Bunny's Wardrobe

Bunny can go bare or bunny can dress up. The
patterns and instructions on the next few pages
give details for making an entire bunny wardrobe:
a reversible vest, stylish felt coat, cross-over
apron, and this season's key accessory – a basket
of felt carrots.

Reversible vest

Make two vests in one with this reversible vest. There are no fastenings, so it is easy to make. Choose thin cotton fabrics: solid for one side and a print or stripe for the other.

YOU WILL NEED
Fabric One
• 6 x 15 inches
Fabric Two
• 6 x 15 inches
• Sewing thread to match fabrics

Preparing patterns Trace or photocopy the pattern twice.

Cut the paper pattern pieces out and join with tape to make a one-piece

vest pattern. The lines of the pattern are the stitching lines; the seam allowances will be added later. Place the two fabrics right sides together, and pin the pattern on top. Mark around the edges with pencil. Remove the pattern, but keep the two fabrics pinned together so they do not slip while being stitched. *Do not cut yet.*

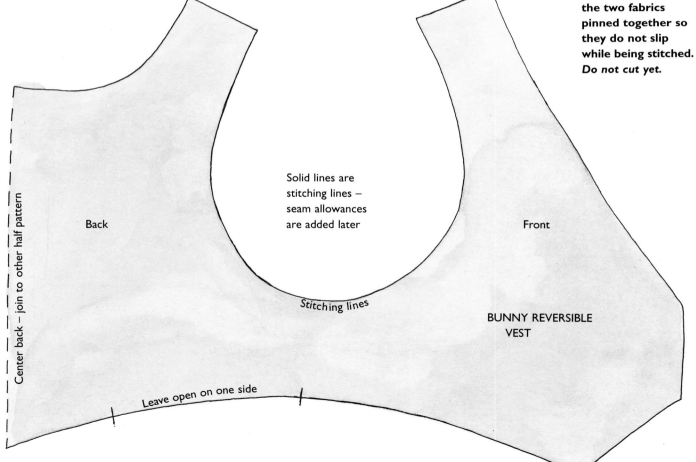

Center back – join to other half pattern

Back

Solid lines are stitching lines — seam allowances are added later

Stitching lines

Front

BUNNY REVERSIBLE VEST

Leave open on one side

Assembly
2 Machine stitch around the lines, leaving an opening in the lower back seam as indicated. Cut the vest out, adding a ¼-inch seam allowance. Clip curved seams and snip off corners.

3 Turn right side out, and carefully push out the corners from the inside with a knitting needle. Press flat, and close the opening with ladder stitch.

4 Try the vest on your bunny. Pin the shoulder seams together by overlapping the front over the back. Stitch neatly in place on both sides. Your vest is now ready and can be worn either side out.

Bunny coat

Bunny's coat is made of felt, a versatile material that does not fray and therefore needs no special finishes on the edges. Felt has no right or wrong side, and there is a huge variety of bright colors to choose from. Choose wool felt if possible, because it is thicker and harder-wearing. Seam allowances of ¼ inch are included where necessary.

These pattern pieces are shown at half size. Draw a grid to double the square size shown and carefully redraw the pieces onto it. If you have access to an enlarging photocopier, set the enlargement to 200% and simply copy the pieces required.

YOU WILL NEED
• 13 x 20-inch piece of felt (preferably made of wool)
• 2 small buttons – gold for preference
• Sewing thread to match fabrics

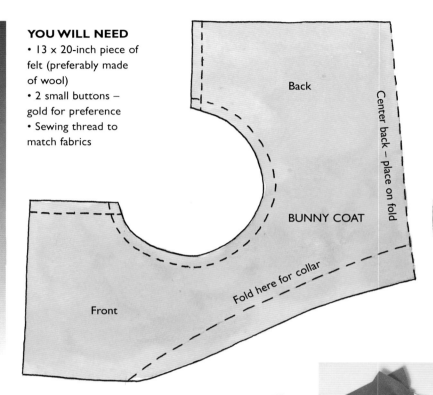

Back

Center back – place on fold

BUNNY COAT

Fold here for collar

Front

BACK

Gathering line

BUNNY COAT SLEEVE

Fold up here for cuffs

FRONT

Preparing patterns
Enlarge pattern pieces (see left). Fold the felt in half and pin the coat pattern to it with the center

back on the fold. Pin the sleeve pattern through both thicknesses to make two sleeves. Cut the pieces out.

Assembly
Gather the curved edge of the sleeve by stitching ¼ inch from the edge. Pull gathers slightly. Fit each sleeve onto the armhole, with the lower curve of the sleeve cap on the front side of the coat. Stitch in place.

5 Stitch the buttons onto one side and make buttonholes to match on the other side. The buttonholes should be smaller than the buttons, as felt stretches easily. A bow tie in matching or contrasting ribbon will go well with the coat.

3 Fold the coat, right sides together, matching underarm seams of coat and sleeves. Pin and stitch; leave a ¼-inch seam. Clip the curved seams under the arms, and press seams open.

4 Turn right side out and try the coat on your bunny. Fold the collar out, and press in place if necessary. Fold the sleeve edges up to make cuffs.

Bow tie

1 Cut 3 inches off the ribbon and set aside. Fold remaining 8 inches, overlapping raw edges at center by ½ inch. Run gathering stitch along center, across the ribbon. Pull to gather and secure with a knot.

2 Make a circle with the thin elastic, overlapping the two ends by ½ inch, and stitch ends together. Attach this seam to the center of the bow, on the side where the raw edges of the ribbon meet.

3 Take the piece of ribbon set aside earlier, and fold it in half lengthwise. Place it around the bow so it covers the gathers and the attached elastic. Fold the piece of ribbon at the back so that the raw edges are hidden, and stitch in place, catching the bow as well so that it cannot slip. With the bow tie under its chin, fluff up the fur at the back of bunny's neck so it covers the elastic.

Bunny apron

A lady bunny will love this apron for working in the yard. It looks very attractive in a striped fabric, but it will also look good in solid or printed fabrics. All pieces have seam allowances included.

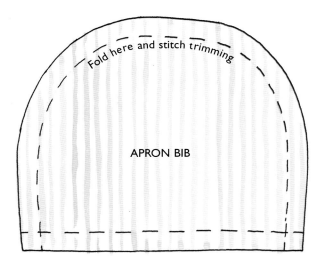

YOU WILL NEED
- 9 x 32 inches of cotton fabric
- 25 inches of 1-inch wide eyelet lace trimming
- Sewing thread to match fabric

Waistband
- 2 x 32 inches

Straps
- two, each 2 x 10 inches

Fold here and stitch trimming

APRON BIB

Seam allowance – ¼in

Preparing patterns Trace or photocopy the pattern for the apron skirt and bib shown full size. You will also need some long strips for the straps and waistband, but no patterns are necessary.

Gather here

Center front – place on fold

APRON SKIRT

Fold here and stitch trimming

2 **Cutting out**
Place the fabric on the table, wrong side up. Measure the waistband strip along one long side of the fabric, mark it, and cut out with scissors, or use a rotary cutter and ruler. Then measure, mark, and cut the two straps in the same way. Pin the bib pattern to the fabric, and cut out. Fold the remaining fabric in half, right sides together. Pin the skirt pattern in place with the center front on the fold, then cut out.

3 **"Press-folding"** Fold up ¼ inch all around the long curved edges of both the bib and skirt. The best way is to press it down, which I like to call "press-fold." Small pleats will form in the seam allowances on the curves, but the eyelet lace trimming will hide these.

4 **Assembly**
Attach the eyelet lace trimming all around the curved edges of the skirt and the bib, with the raw edges on the wrong side, using a top-stitch. Start at one end and stitch as normal on the straight edges, but on the curved areas make small pleats on the trimming to help it go around. You can pin it all first, but it is just as easy to put one pin at the beginning and then guide it gently through the machine.

5 Run two rows of stitching with a long stitch to make gathers along the top edge of the skirt. Do not extend the stitching onto the eyelet lace trimming. Pull the gathers from both ends until the skirt top measures about 6½ inches. Press-fold all the edges of the waistband and the straps, ¼ inch toward the inside. Then press-fold in half, wrong sides together. Stitch the straps closed, all along the three folded edges and the fold, then set aside.

6 Find the center of the waistband and match it to the center of the apron gathers. Push the gathered edge inside the fold of the waistband, and pin in place. Place the bib piece in the center of the band, behind the skirt, and re-pin to hold in place. Topstitch the band to the bib and skirt, and along all four edges of the band to make ties.

7 Stitch one end of each strap to the back of the bib. At the other end, fold back about 2 inches and stitch to the strap to make a loop.

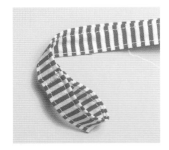

8 Try the apron on the bunny. Cross the straps at the back, slip the ties through the loops, and tie the ends in a bow.

Felt vegetables

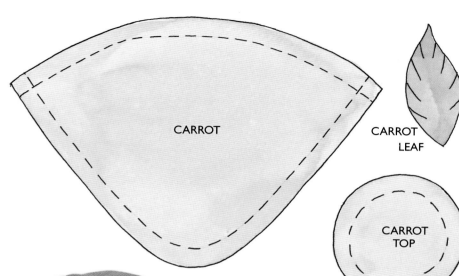

CARROT

CARROT LEAF

CARROT TOP

YOU WILL NEED
- Scraps of felt: reddish-orange and bright green
- A handful of polyester stuffing
- A black permanent felt pen
- Sewing thread to match fabrics

Felt vegetables can easily be made from sewing basket scraps. Here we show how to make a carrot; the same technique can be used for other vegetables.

Make several carrots and other vegetables and put them in a nice basket for your bunny to carry.

1 <u>Making a carrot</u> Trace or photocopy the patterns. Cut one main carrot piece and one top (circle) from orange felt, and two leaves from green felt. Fold the main piece in half, and stitch along the straight side seam, ⅛ inch from the edge.

2 Place the round top on the open circular area of the carrot and stitch together, leaving a small opening. Turn right side out and insert some stuffing, using a knitting needle to push it down. Close the opening with ladder stitch.

3 Snip the sides of the green leaves and ruffle them up. Stitch them together to the center of the carrot top so they stand up. Make a few marks on the orange felt with a black permanent pen to indicate the creases of real carrots.

Bunnies, Bunnies, Bunnies!

There are bunny designs to suit every taste and level of sewing skill. If you're in a hurry for a bunny, make the Clothespin Bunnies on pages 44-45; if you want to show off your technical wizardry, try the Folk Art Bunny; if you're looking for something to amuse your baby, make her a Sock Bunny or a Pocket Bunny.

Pocket bunny

Small enough to sit in your hand or carry with you in your pocket, this bunny is very easy to make. Cotton fabric stitched following a simple one-piece pattern is all that is needed to create your own Pocket Bunny – his arms, legs, and ears are made by stitching separate seams. To make a toy for a young child, embroider the eyes; for an older child or adult, you could stitch on two black beads for extra character. The filling can be polyester wool (the safest for children) or plastic beans – or, as we have used here, a mixture of the two.

YOU WILL NEED

Body
• 7 x 20 inches of cotton fabric

Eyes
• 10 inches black embroidery thread, or 2 x 4mm beads

Nose and mouth
• 10 inches pink embroidery thread

Filling
• ½ ounce polyester stuffing and 2 tablespoons of plastic beads or rice

Ribbon
• 15 inches of ⅜-inch wide
• Sewing thread to match

Pattern pieces Following the instructions for enlarging the pattern piece on page 26, trace or photocopy the paper pattern. Note that the lines are stitching lines; the seam allowances will be added later.

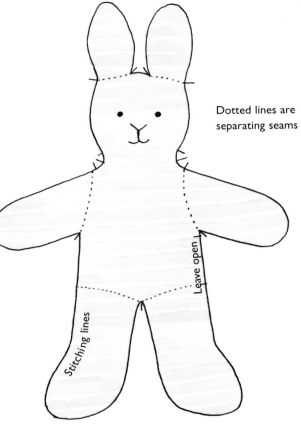

Dotted lines are separating seams

Leave open

Stitching lines

2 Fold the fabric in half, right sides together, and pin the pattern to it. Mark around the edges with pencil or dressmakers' chalk. <u>Do not cut yet.</u> Remove the pattern, but keep the two layers of fabric pinned together. Machine stitch all around on the marked line, leaving an opening below one arm as indicated.

3 Cutting out
Cut the Pocket Bunny out, adding a ¼-inch seam allowance. For ease of turning, clip into the seam allowances at the corners above and below the arms, between the ears, and between the legs. Turn right side out and carefully push out the limbs with a blunt stick.

4 Assembly and stuffing Stitch across the top of the head to separate the ears – these are not stuffed. Stuff the arms and legs with polyester wool, filling the ends of limbs firmly and then loosely nearer the top. Machine stitch the separating lines: first for the arms, from the shoulders to under the arms; and then for legs, from side to side, through the underleg point. Stuff the head and neck very firmly with polyester wool.

5 Now stuff the body with plastic beads or rice, using a small funnel to help keep the beads in check. Do not overfill – it should only be about two-thirds full. Close the opening with ladder stitch, using very small stitches, so the beads or rice cannot escape.

6 Finishing
With doubled black embroidery thread, embroider the eyes halfway down the head, ¾ inch apart, using the pattern as a guide. Alternatively stitch two black beads in place. Embroider the nose with pink thread as shown. Decorate with a ribbon and a bow.

Folk bunny: patterns,

Making a Folk Bunny gives you a wonderful opportunity to experiment with different combinations of fabrics, incorporating bits of lace, ribbons, buttons, raffia, and scraps. And you don't need to worry about finishing seams neatly, as part of the charm of this style is having raw edges. Our Folk Bunny has a big heart.

YOU WILL NEED

Body, ears, and paws
• 10 x 20 inches of unbleached muslin

Clothes
• Cotton fabrics in plaids, prints, solids, geometrics – choose your own individual combination
Sleeves: 6 x 20 inches
Slacks: 9 x 21 inches
Boots: 7 x 9 inches

Heart, bow, and patches
• Small scraps of fabric
• Small scraps of iron-on web bonding material

Trimmings
• 18 inches of thick cotton lace
• 55 inches of very thin ribbon
• 3¾-inch buttons
• Scraps of raffia for hair
• Scrap of sisal string

Features
• Black and red permanent marker pens

Filling
• 4 ounces polyester
• Sewing thread to match

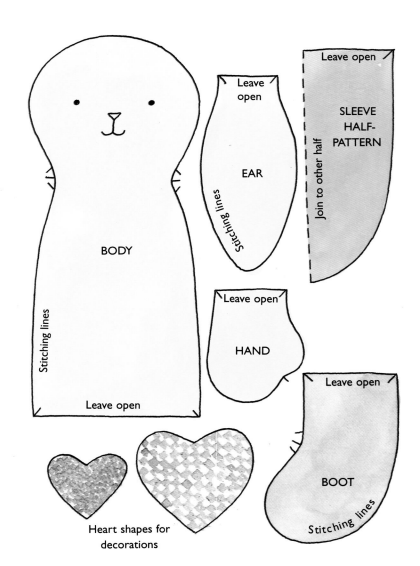

Heart shapes for decorations

Pattern pieces Following the instructions for enlarging the pattern pieces on page 26, trace or photocopy the pattern pieces. The lines are stitching lines unless otherwise indicated, so place the pattern pieces to allow for seam allowances.

marking, and cutting

3 Marking and cutting Fold the sleeve fabric crosswise, right sides together, and similarly mark around the edges of the sleeve pattern piece twice.

5 Prepare the patches by ironing adhesive web bonding material on the back of two scraps of fabric, and cutting out a piece from each, approximately 1½ inches square.

4 Fold the boot fabric lengthwise, right sides together, and mark two boots.

6 Fold the slacks fabric in half, right sides together, and cut along the fold line. Mark and then cut a line 4 inches long from the middle of one shorter side in, for the underleg seam. Turn one slacks piece right side up, remove the paper backing from the patches, and iron them onto one leg. Replace the two slacks pieces, right sides together and underleg cut matching.

2 Fold the muslin in half and pin the pattern pieces for one body, two ears, and two paws to it, and mark around the edges. Do not cut the pieces yet.

Stitching and cutting

1 **Body, ears, and paws** Remove the paper pattern pieces, but keep the two layers of fabric pinned together. Machine stitch on the marked lines, leaving openings where indicated. Cut out, adding ¼-inch seam allowance.

2 **Sleeves** Stitch only along the curved marked lines. Cut out, adding a seam allowance as before.

5 **Turning** Turn all the pieces right side out and push out any seams that need it with a blunt stick.

3 **Slacks** Machine stitch along the two long sides and the underleg seam on both legs with a ¼-inch seam, joining the two leg seams at the crotch. Leave the top and the lower edges of the legs open.

4 **Boots** Stitch around them on the marked lines, leaving the top open. Cut out, adding a seam allowance. For ease of turning, clip the curve.

Stuffing and assembling

1 Boots, body, paws Stuff firmly the boots, the body, and the paws. There is no need to close the openings, as they will be hidden when the clothes are attached.

2 Features Mark two eyes with the black permanent pen and a nose and mouth with the red pen, following the pattern.

3 Ears Press the ears flat. Sew the ears to the head, leaving a 1½-inch space between them at the top of the head.

4 Arms Stuff the arms lightly. Hand gather the bottom edge of each sleeve; insert the open end of one hand, and pull the gathers. Stitch in place, but don't hide the raw edges of the sleeves.

5 Slacks Stuff the slacks legs lightly. Hand gather the lower edges, insert a boot, pull the gathers, and stitch in place as for the paws. Make sure both toes are pointing forward.

6 Gather the top of the slacks and insert the body. Pull the gathers around the neck and stitch in place. Make sure the face and the toes are facing in the same direction.

7 Sleeves Hand stitch the top of each sleeve to each side of the slacks near the neck edge, making sure that the thumbs are facing forward.

Finishing details

How you finish your bunny depends on your taste. This is how to finish our Folk Bunny:

Lace and buttons Attach lace around the neck, wrists, and ankles. Wrap some very narrow ribbon around the wrists and tie a bow.

4 Whiskers For whiskers, unravel a length of sisal, thread some strands through a thick needle, and insert them under the nose.

3 Bows Cut two different-sized strips of fabric for a bow and knot a third strip in the middle. Use raffia for a fringe and hand stitch all these to the head.

2 Stitch buttons on the ankles and neck.

Heart decoration Iron some adhesive web bonding material onto the back of the fabric. Cut around it, pull the paper off, and iron it onto a larger heart shape, cut with pinking shears. With wrong sides facing, stitch together two larger hearts, with a ¼-inch seam. Turn right side out and insert a third heart made of batting. Attach a piece of ribbon, folded in half, with the long ends going up; make a bow and stitch it to the neck.

Sock bunny: mark & stitch

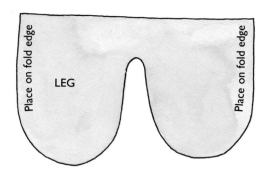

ARM — Place on fold edge

LEG — Place on fold edge — Place on fold edge

EARS — Place on fold edge — Place on fold edge

YOU WILL NEED

Body
• One sock; here we have used a child's cotton sock (age 2-3 years)

Eyes
• 1 yard black embroidery thread

Nose and mouth
• 1 yard pale pink embroidery thread

Filling
• 1 ounce polyester
• Strong sewing thread for separation ties

Decorations
• Ribbon

Sock Bunny is an ideal soft toy for a small child. It is easily made with any kind of sock – the templates can be adapted to the sock size. For safety reasons, you should embroider the eyes and limit decorations to ribbons.

Marking and stitching Prepare the templates by tracing or photocopying the patterns shown full size; make two arm templates. If you are using a different size sock, you may have to enlarge or reduce the templates.

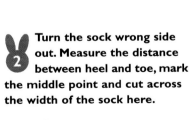

2 Turn the sock wrong side out. Measure the distance between heel and toe, mark the middle point and cut across the width of the sock here.

3 Open out the main piece of the sock sideways so that the heel is at the back. Place the ear template ¼ inch down from the top and the leg template ¼ inch from the cut edge, and pin them in place. As it is difficult to mark a knitted surface with a pencil, keep the templates pinned to the sock and stitch

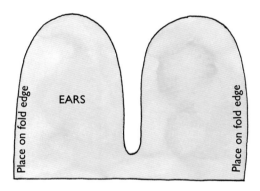

along the curved edge of each template, following the edge of the paper. Open out the

toe piece of the sock as above and place the two arm templates, one reversed, each with one edge on the fold side. Pin the templates in place and stitch following the edge of the paper.

Cutting and stuffing

The art of stuffing

The shape of a toy can be guided and modified by manipulating the stuffing:

• Use your hands from the outside while stuffing the toy to give it the desired shape.

• Stuffing can be moved along by inserting a large thick needle into the toy and using it as a lever to move the filling.

• Toys take a lot more stuffing than you think – a rule of thumb is put in as much as you can, then add 50 percent.

• Stuffing can be pushed through very small openings; you can start closing the opening and then add filling through the last ½ inch of space.

1 Cutting Cut around the stitched shapes, adding a seam allowance of between ⅛ inch and ¼ inch, according to the space available.

2 Make a small vertical cut of approximately 1 inch on the heel side of the sock, just above the center of the legs, and turn the sock right side out through it. Be careful not to stretch it too much or it may snag, although it is amazing how small a hole you need to turn things right side out.

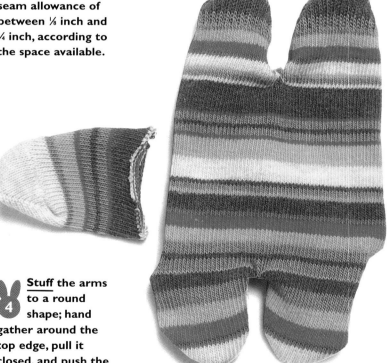

4 Stuff the arms to a round shape; hand gather around the top edge, pull it closed, and push the edges in. Stitch the gathers securely in place.

3 Stuffing Stuff the legs to a round shape. Do not stuff the ears; stuff the top third of the sock to make a nice round head; stuff the rest of the sock for the body. Close the opening with ladder stitch.

Assembling and finishing

1 Neck Take a length of strong sewing thread in a matching color and wrap around the sock two or three times, a third down from where the ears start, to make the neck. Knot firmly in place.

2 Arms Attach the arms to the side of the body, near the neck, by ladder stitching around the gathered end onto the body.

3 Legs Tie each separately in the same way.

4 Ears Tie the ears, both together, on top of the head.

5 Features Make the eyes either by embroidering them with black embroidery thread or stitching on two buttons, halfway down the face and 2 inches apart. Embroider the nose and mouth with pink embroidery thread as shown. Hide any knots in the neck.

6 Finishing touches Decorate with a ribbon tied around the neck.

Clothespin bunnies

Old-fashioned wooden clothespins can make attractive little bunnies. Here are a couple of Clothespin Bunnies with long ears dressed in pieces of ribbon.

Place on fold

EAR

PAW

YOU WILL NEED
Old-fashioned wooden clothespins
• One per bunny
Ears and paws
• Scraps of unbleached muslin
Clothes
• 2-inch wide ribbon: 15 inches for dress; 9 inches for suit
Trimmings
• Scraps of lace, thin ribbon, felt, and small beads
Features
• Black and red permanent marker pens
• Thick white glue
• Tweezers to help assemble the clothes

Pattern pieces and features Trace or photocopy ear and paw pattern pieces shown full size. Cut two paws per bunny, and one set of ears on the fold (they are joined together at the top). Draw a face on each bunny following the illustration – you can use black pen only, or black and red pens. Draw some whiskers if desired.

Bunny with dress

1 **Assemble** Wrap a 2½-inch piece of ribbon around the body and glue at the back.

2 For each sleeve cut a 2¼-inch length of ribbon. Stitch the raw ends together, gather both ends, and insert a muslin paw into one end; stitch in place. Pull gathers on the other end, knot, and glue to the body near the neck.

5 Glue the ears to the top of the head and decorate with a piece of thin ribbon, knotted to simulate a bow.

4 When the glue is dry, gather some lace, pull the gathers, and wrap around neck; knot in place.

3 Cut a 7-inch length of ribbon and join ends together. Hand gather the circumference, pull gathers to fit waist, and knot. Glue skirt to waist.

Bunny with suit

1 **Assembly** Cut two pieces of ribbon, each 2 inches long. Wrap around the legs and glue them in the space between them – use tweezers to help.

2 To make the jacket, wrap a 2½-inch piece of ribbon around the body. Glue at the back.

3 Wrap some thin ribbon around the neck; cut ½ inch of thin ribbon, gather in the center, and glue to the neck for a bow tie. Stitch three small beads onto the jacket for buttons.

4 To make each sleeve, wrap a 1-inch piece of ribbon around a muslin paw and either stitch or glue together. Glue the tops of the arms to the body near the neck.

5 Use a suitable-sized coin as a template to cut a circle of felt for the hat rim. Cut between two and four smaller circles for the hat top and glue them together, then glue them onto the brim. Glue the ears onto the bunny and glue the hat on top.

Clothespin bunny variations
• **Clothespin Bunnies'** clothes can be made with thin cotton fabric instead of ribbon. Choose solid fabrics, small prints, thin stripes or small geometrics to keep in scale.
• **Using different fabric colors and dimensions, other looks can be achieved:** for example, longer or shorter skirts and tops; and two-tone costumes.
• **For footwear, the lower end of the "legs" can be painted brown or black with acrylic paints before dressing the bunny.**
• **Other accessories can be made with bits of felt, trimming, and tiny beads:** for example, necklaces, shoulder bags, vests, etc.

A bevy of bunnies

Bunnies come in all shapes and sizes – small or big, long or short limbs, ears up or down. They can be made from fur fabric, soft fleece, velvet, or calico. They can be realistic or stylized, rabbit-like or doll-like, bare or dressed.

This bunny is a well-loved one – you can detect it in its worn fur, and guess it from its friendly expression.

This furry bunny wears cotton slacks, a bright red cap, and a school bag – but it looks as if it's fallen asleep on the way to school!

An angel bunny in muslin, wearing a dress, and with stylized features; an unusual toy or decorative addition to an older child's room.

A velvet bunny with prominent white teeth and strong whiskers. It is made from the same pattern as the Kit Bunny, with the addition of extra seam allowances.

A sleepy, cuddly bunny with floppy ears and bent legs, waiting for a friendly owner to give a good home.

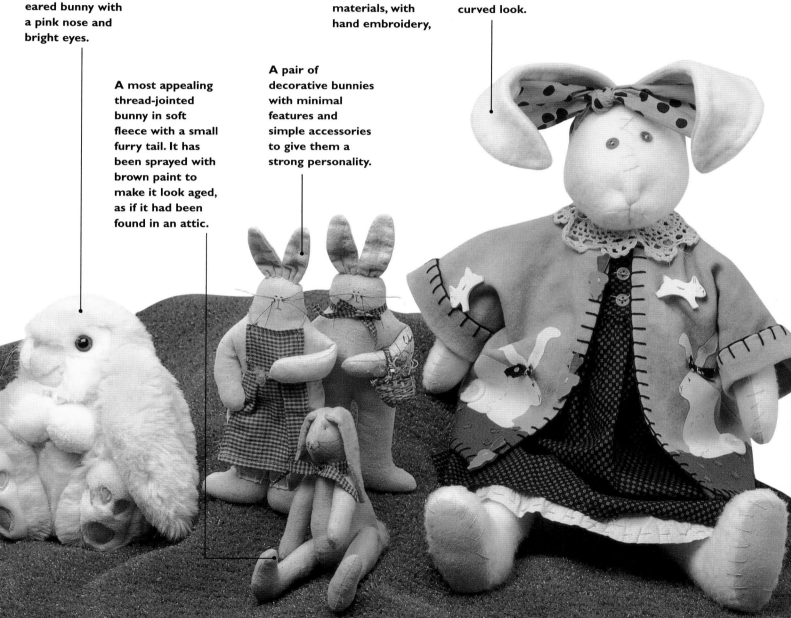

A sweet little lop-eared bunny with a pink nose and bright eyes.

A most appealing thread-jointed bunny in soft fleece with a small furry tail. It has been sprayed with brown paint to make it look aged, as if it had been found in an attic.

A pair of decorative bunnies with minimal features and simple accessories to give them a strong personality.

Large artist-made bunny doll, beautifully dressed in natural materials, with hand embroidery,

bunny badges, and button eyes. Its ears are wired to achieve an unusual curved look.

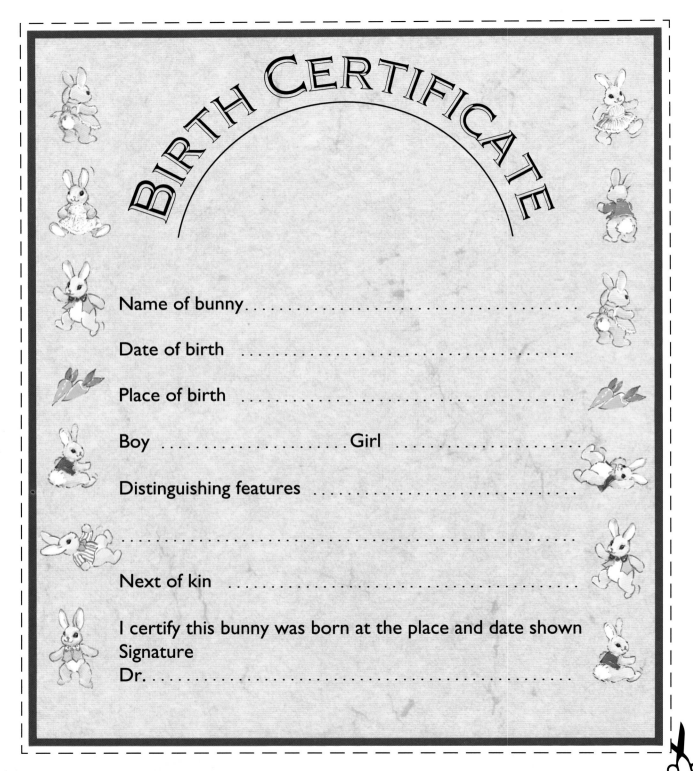

BIRTH CERTIFICATE

Name of bunny...

Date of birth ....

Place of birth ....

Boy ....Girl ....

Distinguishing features ....

....

Next of kin ....

I certify this bunny was born at the place and date shown
Signature
Dr. ....